THE QUEEN WHO RULED

FOR 44 YEARS

BIOGRAPHY OF QUEEN ELIZABETH 1

CHILDREN'S BIOGRAPHY BOOKS

Queen Elizabeth was the Queen of England for 44 years. She was born in Greenwich, England on September 7, 1533, and died in Richmond, England on March 24, 1603. She was also known by her nicknames of The Virgin Queen and Good Queen Bess.

GROWING UP AS PRINCESS ELIZABETH

Princess Elizabeth was born to Henry VIII, the King of England and Queen Anne, as heir to England's throne. She was named after her two grandmothers, both named Elizabeth.

Portrait of Elizabeth I as a 14-year-old princess

KING HENRY VIII WANTED A SON

King Henry wanted a son, not a daughter. He wanted a son to be his heir and reign as king one day. He had wanted a son so much that he proceeded to divorce Catherine, his first wife, when she didn't produce a son. When Elizabeth was only 3, her father had Queen Anne, her mother, killed because she didn't produce a son. Elizabeth was then declared illegitimate, depriving her a place in royal succession. He then married Jane who was finally able to produce a son for him, Prince Edward. Unfortunately, she died during the birth of Prince Edward. He then married Anne of Cleves, Catherine Howard, and Catherine Parr.

King Henry VIII portrait

He then suffered a leg injury during a jousting match in 1536. Because of this injury, it was difficult for him to move around. He then became very overweight and his skin became covered with boils, which are painful infections. In 1547, he died at 55, and Prince Edward succeeded him, becoming King Edward VI.

NO LONGER A PRINCESS

Once the king was married again she no longer was the heir to the throne, or a princess. She moved in with Edward, her half-brother, and still managed to live like a king's daughter. She had people to take care of her and tutors who assisted with her education. She was intelligent and successfully learned reading and writing in several different languages. She learned to sew as well as how to play a virginal, which is similar to a piano.

Queen Elizabeth I - This is the earliest full-length portrait of the queen, made before the emergence of symbolic portraits representing the iconography of the "Virgin Queen"

Her father's last wife, Catherine Parr, was gentle with Elizabeth. She assured Elizabeth grew up in the Protestant faith and that she had the best tutors.

KATHARINE PARRE

KING HENRY DIES

When she was only 13, her father passed away. The throne was left to his son Edward. He did, however, leave her with a sizeable income to live on. As Edward reigned as king, she lived and enjoyed life as a wealthy lady.

Edward as Prince of Wales, 1546. He wears the Prince of Wales's feathers and crown on the pendant jewel.

THOMAS SEYMOUR

Once Henry VIII passed away, his widow, Catherine Parr, wed Thomas Seymour of Sudeley. The couple decided to take Elizabeth into their home in Chelsea. Elizabeth experienced an emotional crisis that may have affected the rest of her lifetime

Portrait of Thomas Seymour, 1st Baron Seymour of Sudeley

Thomas engaged in inappropriate horseplay and romps with Elizabeth who was only 14 at the time. Rather than confronting her husband about this, Parr began to join in. Once Parr found Thomas and Elizabeth embracing, she ended this by sending Elizabeth away in 1548.

Thomas continued to scheme for control over the royal family and attempted to be appointed as governor. Parr died on September 5, 1548 during childbirth and he again directed his attention to Elizabeth, and planned to marry her. The details of his prior behavior were revealed, and for the king's council and for his brother, this was it.

Queen Elizabeth I and Leicester

SINE SOLE
IRIS.

Seymour was then arrested in January of 1549 for allegedly plotting to wed Elizabeth and takeover as the Lord Protector. Elizabeth admitted to nothing. This exasperated Sir Robert Tyrwhitt, her interrogator, who went on to report, "I do see it in her face that she is guilty." On March 20, 1549, Seymour was beheaded.

Queen Elizabeth I. The "Rainbow Portrait", c. 1600

Tower of London

THE QUEEN'S SISTER

King Edward soon became ill and passed away when he was 15. Mary, her half-sister then became the Queen. As a devout Catholic, Mary demanded all of England to switch to the Catholic religion. If anyone didn't, they were jailed or killed. Mary also wed Philip, a Spanish prince.

Mary I of England

Queen Mary was not liked by the English. She soon became concerned that Elizabeth might try to take over the throne. She proceeded to jail Elizabeth since she was a Protestant and Elizabeth spent two months at the Tower of London in a jail cell.

Hatfield House - It was here that Elizabeth was told of her sister's death in November 1558.

BECOMING QUEEN OF ENGLAND

When Mary died, Elizabeth had been under house arrest. Within a few moments of Mary's death, Elizabeth went from being a prisoner in a jail cell to becoming the Queen of England. On January 15, 1559, she was crowned as the Queen of England at the age of 25.

Queen Elizabeth I of England in her coronation robes, patterned with Tudor roses and trimmed with ermine

MARRIAGE QUESTION

From the beginning of her reign, it had been expected that she would get married and the question was to whom she would marry. She had received several offers of marriage, but never accepted any proposals and never had any children; it is not clear why. It has been speculated by historians that Thomas Seymour had ruined her idea of a sexual relationship, or that she may have been infertile.

She considered several suitors until the age of approximately 50. Francis, Duke of Anjou was her last relationship, and he was 22 years younger than she was. While marriage included the risk of loss of power similar to her sister, marriage offered the possibility of an heir. The choice for husband, however, could also possibly provoke political instability or insurrection.

John Dee performing an experiment before Queen Elizabeth I.

LIFE AS A QUEEN

She worked hard and wanted to be a good queen. She tried to keep the people of England safe and would visit different cities and towns in England. She started the Privy Council, which was a council of advisors. This Council assisted her when she had to deal with different countries, taking care of dire issues, and working with their army. Her Secretary of State, William Cecil, was her most trusted advisor.

The Wanstead or Welbeck Portrait of Elizabeth I or The Peace Portrait of Elizabeth I

She became ill with smallpox in 1562, but unlike others who died because of this disease, she was able to survive it.

Elizabeth enjoyed wearing fancy gowns as Queen. The style of the era soon followed, full of braids, ruffles, intricate embroidery, wide sleeves, and plenty of jewels.

PLOTS AGAINST THE QUEEN

While she was queen, several people had attempted to have her assassinated so they could take over the throne. Included in this list was Queen Mary of Scots, her cousin, who had attempted to have her killed many times. Eventually, she had her apprehended and put to death

S o as to find out who was conspiring against her, she
started a network of spies throughout England. Sir
Francis Walsingham, a member of the Privy Council, ran
her network of spies.

Elizabeth I and the Spanish Armada, an unsigned painting mistakenly attributed to Nicholas Hilliard, oil on canvas.

WAR WITH SPAIN

She tried to avoid fighting wars and really didn't want to conquer any other countries. She simply wanted England to prosper and be safe. The King of Spain was not happy when she had Queen Mary of Scots killed and sent a fleet of warships known as the Spanish Armada, to take over England.

English ships and the Spanish Armada, August 1588

The English navy, being outgunned, was able to set afire many of ships of the Armada. A bad storm then struck the Armada, causing many of their remaining ships to sink. Somehow, England conquered and less than half of the Armada returned to Spain.

Queen Elizabeth I preceded by the Knights of the Garter.

THE ELIZABETHAN AGE

England was ushered into the age of expansion, peace, and prosperity once they defeated Spain. This time period is also famous for the thriving English Theatre, in particular William Shakespeare, the playwright. It also became a time for exploration as well as expansion of this Empire to the New World.

The Elizabethan Era occurring from 1558 through 1603 and is considered as the golden age of English History by many historians. The era was named for Queen Elizabeth I.

WILLIAM SHAKESPEARE

William Shakespeare was a playwright, baptized on April 26, 1564 in Stratford-upon-Avon, England, but may have been born on April 23, 1564. He passed away in Stratford-upon-Avon, England on April 23, 1616. He was known for authoring plays included Macbeth, Hamlet, and Romeo and Juliet.

William Shakespeare portrait

He was considered by several to be the best author of the English language, and one of the more influential. He is credited, through his works, with the introduction of almost 3,000 words to the English language. Also, following the Bible, his works are the most quoted.

William Shakespeare's birthplace

HER DEATH

She passed away March 24, 1603 and was then buried at Westminster Abby. Her coffin was moved downriver to Whitehall at night on a barge that was lit up with torches. On April 28, her coffin was later carried to Westminster Abbey via a hearse which was drawn by four horses that had black velvet hung over their backs.

Westminister Abbey cathedral in London, United Kingdom

James VI of Scotland was her successor. As her reign came to an end, the city of London had a population of approximately 200,000.

Now that you have learned about Queen Elizabeth I, there is much more to learn about the Elizabethan Age, and the kings and queens during this time period. For additional information, go to your local library, research the internet, and ask questions of your teachers, family, and friends.

Visit
BABY PROFESSOR
EDUCATION KIDS
www.BabyProfessorBooks.com
to download Free Baby Professor eBooks
and view our catalog of new and exciting
Children's Books